Buzz and Zip

by Tamera Williams
illustrated by Kersti Frigell

Core Decodable 31

McGraw Hill Education

Bothell, WA • Chicago, IL • Columbus, OH • New York, NY

MHEonline.com

Send all inquiries to:
McGraw-Hill Education
8787 Orion Place
Columbus, OH 43240

ISBN: 978-0-02-139002-1
MHID: 0-02-139002-9

Printed in the United States of America.

9 10 11 KOD 24

Zack is in a hat of fuzz.

Zack is in lots of fuzz.

Zack is in back of Liz.

Zack asks lots of stuff.

"Can I buzz? Can I zip?" Zack asks.

"What can buzz and zip?" asks Liz.

Zack the bug can!